Th

My name, My joke

belongs to

_____

Also in Red Fox by Jennifer and Graeme Curry

MY NAME, MY POEM

MY NAME, MY JOKE

Jennifer Curry

Illustrated by Harry Venning

RED FOX

A Red Fox Book
Published by Arrow Books Limited
20 Vauxhall Bridge Road, London SW1V 2SA

An imprint of the Random Century Group

London Melbourne Sydney Auckland
Johannesburg and agencies throughout the world

Red Fox Edition 1990

First published 1988

Set in Century Schoolbook
by JH Graphics Ltd, Reading

Made and printed in Great Britain by
Courier International, Tiptree, Essex

ISBN 0 09 968 690 2

This book is dedicated to:

Polly, Rose, Oliver, Annie, William, Ned, Theo, Eliza, Emer, Lily, Edward and Alexander. . . but most of all to their grandmother, my best-of-friends and fellow-joker, Anne Girling

A

Knock! Knock!
Who's there?
ABBY.
Abby who?
'Abby birthday to you, 'abby birthday to you . . .

Who do you get if you cross a large church with a high wind?
ABIGAIL.

Who was the fastest runner ever?
ADAM. He was the first in the Human Race.

Knock! Knock!
Who's there?
ADELAIDE.
Adelaide who?
Adelaide an egg if I'd laughed any more.

ADRIAN'S rather portly.
  He's got a bulgy tum.
He's coming over shortly –
  But you'll never see him run.

Knock! Knock!
Who's there?
ALAN.
Alan who?
Alan'swer that when you open the door.

Knock! Knock!
Who's there?
ALEC.
Alec who?
Alec of paint is what this place needs.

Knock! Knock!
Who's there?
ALEX.
Alex who?
Alex – plain later. Just open the door!

What do you call the girl with a creepy crawlie on
her head?
ALICE.

8

Knock! Knock!
Who's there?
ALI.
Ali who?
Ali time you knew it was me.

Knock! Knock!
Who's there?
ALISON.
Alison who?
Alison to my radio every day.

Who do you get if you cross a narrow street with a flight of steps?
ALISTAIR.

Knock! Knock!
Who's there?
ALTHEA.
Althea who?
Althea when you open thith door!

Knock! Knock!
Who's there?
AMANDA.
Amanda who?
A man demanding to see you.

A furious father walked into school and demanded to see his daughter's teacher.

'Why did you give my little AMY minus one for her exam?' he asked.

'Well,' said the teacher, 'the only thing she wrote was her name – and she managed to spell that wrong!'

Knock! Knock!
Who's there?
ANDY.
Andy who?
And he gone and hit me again.

Knock! Knock!
Who's there?
ANATOLE.
Anatole who?
Anatole him what I thought of him!

Find the hidden name:
'What I like best is strawberry jam and real butter on my bread.'
                    Answer – *ANDREA*.

Knock! Knock!
Who's there?
ANNE.
Anne who?
Another twit like you.

Knock! Knock!
Who's there?
ANNIE.
Annie who?
Annie – body alive in there?

What did the fisherman call his twins?
ANNETTE and ROD.

What do you call the boy with the insect on his leg?
ANTONY.

Knock! Knock!
Who's there?
ARMAND.
Armand who?
Armand the outside trying to get inside!

ASHLEY and ANGELA went out to a restuarant for supper. After they had finished they went to the cashdesk and Angela paid what she owed. But Ashley wrote on a piece of paper 1004180, and showed it to the cashier. 'No charge' said the cashier. Why do you think Ashley was able to walk out without paying?

> **Answer** – The number was a code. It meant 'I owe nothing for I ate nothing'.

Knock! Knock!
Who's there?
AVIS.
Avis who?
Avis just passing so I thought I'd give you a knock.

B

What do you call the girl with the comb and scissors on her head?
BARBARA.

Knock! Knock!
Who's there?
BARBIE.
Barbie who?
Barbie-Q-Chicken special delivery. It's finger lickin' good!

BARRY's got a girl-friend
Barry's quite a dish
I saw them down the High Street
Eating chips – AND fish!

What do you call the girl with the stop-watch on her head?
BE-A-TRICE.

What do you call the girl who conjures with beer glasses?
BEATRIX.

THE AMAZING BEATRIX

Knock! Knock!
Who's there?
BEN an' ANNA.
Ben an' Anna who?
Ben an' Anna split so I screamed.

Knock! Knock!
Who's there?
BENNY.
Benny who?
Benny long time no see.

Knock! Knock!
Who's there?
BERYL.
Beryl who?
Beryl-load of monkeys.

Knock! Knock!
Who's there?
BETH.
Beth who?
Beth wishesth, thweetie!

When is a copper not a copper?
When he's a BOBBY.

Two young girls were seated at t.
Discussing the things that might b.
 'I think I'll wed BILLY.'
  said MOLLY TO MILLY,
'That is, if he asks me, you c.'

Oh, sad is that youngster called BRIAN,
A-moppin' his eyes and a cryin'.
    He's swallowed his parrot
    Instead of a carrot.
And it feels like his parrot is dyin'

What do you call the girl who builds roads across rivers?
BRIDGET.

Knock! Knock!
Who's there?
BRUCE.
Bruce who?
Careful – I Bruce easily.

C

Knock! Knock!
Who's there?
CANDICE.
Candice who?
Candice be love?

What do you call a learner-driver going backwards?
CAR-L.

Who do you get if you cross a motor with a note of music?
CAR-LA

Find the hidden name:
'You can't drive a car lying on the back seat.'
Answer – CARLY

Knock! Knock!
Who's there?
CARMEN
Carmen who?
I'm Carmen in the window if you don't open the door!

What do you call the girl singing a Christmas song?
CAROL.

Who do you get if you cross a Christmas song with a telephone wire?
CAROLINE.

What do you call the girl with a basket on her head?
CARRIE.

What do you call the girl who liked to mess about on her daddy's 'yacht'?
Answer – *CATHY*.

Knock! Knock!
Who's there?
CELESTE.
Celeste who?
Celeste time I saw a face like yours I was at the zoo!

Knock! Knock!
Who's there?
CELIA.
Celia who?
Celia later, alligator!

Who do you get if you cross a cleaning lady with the Tower of Pisa?
CHARLENE.

CHARLES is a Royal, of stature and poise,
But sometimes he'd love to be one of the boys!

What do you call the girl with the bucket and broom on her head?
CHARLOTTE.

Knock! Knock!
Who's there?
CHER.
Cher who?
Cherlock Holmes, Sherlock's little sister.

Knock! Knock!
Who's there?
CHRIS.
Chris who?
Christmas comes but once a year.

Knock! Knock!
Who's there?
CHRISTINE.
Christine who?
Onward Christine Soldiers.

What do you call the Yorkshire lass with the cream cake on her head?
Eeh! CLAIRE.

What do you call the girl with the eagle on her head?
CLAUDIA.

What do you call the boy with a seagull on his head?
CLIFF.

Find the hidden name:
Hurry, I need help. Does the doc live here?
Answer – CLIVE.

Knock! Knock!
Who's there?
COLIN.
Colin who?
Colin the doctor – I've caught my death of cold out here.

What do you call the girl with an apple peeler on her head?
CORA.

Knock! Knock!
Who's there?
COSMO.
Cosmo who?
You Cosmo trouble than anyone I know!

Said young CRAIG, in his hot air ballon,
'I shall see all the stars very soon,'
  Craig was right, for he dropped
  And he saw, where he stopped,
Three million bright stars, and a moon.

Knock! Knock!
Who's there?
CY.
Cy who?
Cy-in' and sobbin' cos you won't let me in.

D

How can the 'maiden' be turned into a boy?
Answer – *DAMIEN*.

There once was a fellow called DANIEL.
Who bought a young brown and white spaniel.
   The dog was a pet
   But it swallowed the vet
And that was a problem for Daniel.

Knock! Knock!
Who's there?
DANIELLE.
Danielle who?
Danielle at me, I heard you the first time.

Knock! Knock!
Who's there?
DARREN.
Darren who?
Darren't tell you.

Find the hidden name:
'He entered, avid for food.'
        Answer – *DAVID*.

What do you call the girl with the sunrise in her eyes?
DAWN.

The day after he got his school report DEREK went to see his teacher. 'I don't want to worry you, Miss,' said Derek, 'but my Dad says that if I don't get better marks soon somebody's going to get a good spanking.'

Knock! Knock!
Who's there?
DEAN.
Dean who?
De'an not know my name yet?

Knock! Knock!
Who's there?
DEBBIE.
Debbie who?
De bee sting but de butterfly don't!

What do you call the girl with a pack of cards on her head?
DELIA.

Who do you get if you cross a lion's lair with a pair of leg joints?
DENISE.

Knock! Knock!
Who's there?
DEXTER.
Dexter who?
Dexter halls with boughs of holly.

A singer whose name was DIANA
Was caught in a flood in Havana.
    She floated away,
      While her boyfriend, called JAY,
Accompanied her on the piana.

Knock! Knock!
Who's there?
DIANE.
Diane who?
Di-ane a friend have come for tea.

Knock! Knock!
Who's there?
DINAH.
Dinah who?
I don't know but Dinah might!

What do you call the boy with a pile of stolen dominoes?
DOMINIC.

What do you call the boy who nods upside down?
DON.

I yelled, 'Hello there, DONNA.'
She bashed me on the head!
'My real name is MADONNA –
Don't shorten it,' she said.

What do you call the girl standing on the horizon?
DOT.

What do you call the boy with the spade in his head?
DOUG.

What do you call the boy without the spade in his head?
DOUGLAS.

E

Knock! Knock!
Who's there?
EARL.
Earl who?
Earl tell you when you open the door.

What do you call the boy with a wooden head?
EDWARD.

What do you call the girl who stands on one leg
all day long?
EILEEN.

Knock! Knock!
Who's there?
ELAINE.
Elaine who?
Eel ain't a tasty fish to eat with chips!

TEACHER: Eleanor, you can't sleep in class
ELEANOR: *No, but if you didn't talk so loud, I
could.*

Knock! Knock!
Who's there?
ELIZA.
Eliza who?
'Ere lies a friend worn out with knocking on your door.

One day ELIZABETH woke up to find an elephant sitting on her head. She rushed to the doctor's surgery.

'Gosh!' said the doctor. 'You really need help.'

'I certainly do,' said the elephant. 'Get this girl out from under me.'

What two letters make a girl's name?
L.N. (or I.V.)

Knock! Knock!
Who's there?
ELOISE.
Eloise who?
'Ello, ees any one at 'ome?

Knock! Knock!
Who's there?
ELSIE.
Elsie who?
Elsie you later.

Knock! Knock!
Who's there?
EMER.
Emer who?
Emergency exit this way — the house is burning
down.

EMILY, Emily, daughter dear,
Why do you get up so late?
Your breakfast was on the hob, you know,
But now it's stuck to the plate!

Knock! Knock!
Who's there?
EMMA.
Emma who?
Emma-mazed the way you keep me waiting.

Knock! Knock!
Who's there?
ENA.
Ena who?
Enough's as good as a feast.

ERICA, Erica's gone to America,
Gone on the Greyhound bus.
She'd better come back or she'll get the sack –
And her boyfriend is making a fuss.

Knock! Knock!
Who's there?
EVAN.
Evan who?
Evan't seen you for ages.

F

Knock! Knock!
Who's there?
FANNY.
Fanny who?
Fanny-body calls, I'm out!

Knock! Knock!
Who's there?
FELIX.
Felix who?
Felix my ice
cream I'll lick
his.

What do you call the girl with a tub of margarine
on her head?
FLORA.

Knock! Knock!
Who's there?
FRANCES.
Frances who?
France's capital city is called Paris.

Knock! Knock!
Who's there?
FRANK.
Frank who?
Frank. N. Stein – Yarrgh!

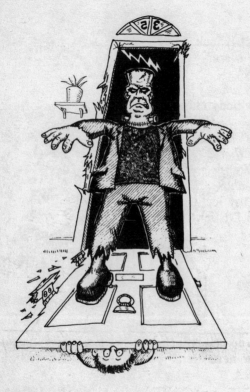

Knock! Knock!
Who's there?
FIONA
Fiona who?
Fiona-d a telephone, I wouldn't have to knock.

G

What do you call the girl with the wind in her hair?
GALE.

GARETH and GAVIN got a sledge for Christmas. Gareth came in crying.

'Now, Gavin,' said their father, 'I told you you had to share the sledge with Gareth.'

'I *am* sharing it,' said Gavin, 'I have it going *down* the hills, and he has it coming *up*.'

What boy is coloured 'gray'?

        Answer – *GARY*.

What do you call the mother with a precious jewel on her head?
GEMMA.

Oh GENEVIEVE! Can you believe
She keeps a beetle up her sleeve
And calls him ALEXANDER!

GILLIAN went to the dentist's.

'Oh dear!' said the dentist, peering at her bad tooth. 'That's the worst cavity I've ever seen! Ever seen! Ever seen!'

'I heard the first time,' said Gillian. 'There's no need to repeat yourself.'

'I didn't,' said the dentist. 'That was the echo.'

GRAHAM had just finished his very first day at school.

'What did you learn today?' his mother asked him.

'Not enough,' said Graham. 'I've got to go back again tomorrow.'

Knock! Knock!
Who's there?
GUS.
Gus who?
That's what YOU're supposed to do!

What do you call the boy with a bonfire on his head?
GUY.

H

There once was a young man called HANK
Who invented a new kind of tank.
  He said it would float,
  Just like a boat –
But the first time he tried it, it sank.

A girl I met once was called HANNAH.
She slipped on the peel of a 'nana.
  The words she let pass,
  As she fell on the grass,
Did *not* please her poppa or mamma.

Knock! Knock!
Who's there?
HANS.
Hans who?
Hans up! I'm a burglar.

Knock! Knock!
Who's there?
HARRIET.
Harriet who?
Harriet my sticky bun.

Knock! Knock!
Who's there?
HARRY.
Harry who?
Harry on down.

Knock! Knock!
Who's there?
HARVEY.
Harvey who?
Harvey going to play this stupid 'Knock! Knock!'
all day?

Knock! Knock!
Who's there?
HAYLEY.
Hayley who?
Hey! Lean out of the window and open this door.

What do you call a round, brown, shiny nutter?
HAZEL.

Knock! Knock!
Who's there?
HEDDA.
Hedda who?
Hedda feeling you wouldn't open the door.

Find the hidden name:
'The length of your hair is a disgrace.'
Answer – *HELEN*

What *did* you call the girl with a bloodthirsty
brother on her head?
HENRIETTA.

Have you heard of HESTER?
    Say it in a whisper.
    We know her friends all missed her.
'Cos she ran away to Leicester.

Knock! Knock!
Who's there?
HOWARD.
Howard who?
Howard I know?

Knock! Knock!
Who's there?
HUGH.
Hugh who?
Don't just shout 'yoo-hoo' – open this door.

Knock! Knock!
Who's there?
HUGO
Hugo who?
Hugo-ing to come out today?

I

Knock! Knock!
Who's there?
IAN.
Ian who?
'E an' me.

Knock! Knock!
Who's there?
IDA.
Ida who?
Ida know. I forgot. Sorry!

Knock! Knock!
Who's there?
IONA.
Iona who?
Iona have eyes for you!

Knock! Knock!
Who's there?
IRA.
Ira who?
Ira-turn with yet another 'Knock! Knock!' joke.

Knock! Knock!
Who's there?
ISABEL.
Isabel who?
Is a bell necessary on a bike?

Knock! Knock!
Who's there?
IVAN.
Ivan who?
Ivan infectious disease. (SLAM!)

Knock! Knock!
Who's there?
IVOR.
Ivor who?
Ivor good mind not to tell you!

What do you call the girl who keeps climbing up the wall?
IVY.

J

What do you call the boy with a car on his head?
JACK.

TEACHER: JAMES, can you explain how you have
  exactly the same answers as SHANE?
JAMES: *Please sir, Shane and me were sharing
  the same pencil.*

Knock! Knock!
Who's there?
JANET
Janet who?
Janet know I've been knocking on this door for
ages?

DINNER LADY: What's your name, little girl?
SCHOOLGIRL: *JAQUELINE.*
DINNER LADY: Well, Jaqueline, if you don't stop
  coming back here for seconds we'll have to call
  you Jaquefat!

Who do you get if you cross a boy with a brightly-
feathered bird?
JASON.

What did the doctor say to the District Nurse?
Hi! JEAN.

JEFFREY went to see the doctor.

'I can't sleep,' he said. 'My little sister JANE thinks she's a refrigerator.'

'But how does that stop you from sleeping?' asked the doctor.

'Jane sleeps with her mouth open,' explained Jeffrey, 'and that little light keeps me awake all night.'

What does Jenny call her fake fur coat?
JENNIFER.

Knock! Knock!
Who's there?
JENNY
Jenny who?
Jenny'd any help in there?

There was a young fellow called JEREMY
Who said to the boatman, 'Please ferry me'.
　　But the boat sprung a leak.
　　Quite unable to speak,
Glug-glug-glug, glug-*glug*-glug,' gasped Jeremy,

Knock! Knock!
Who's there?
JESS.
Jess who?
Jess me and my shadow.

Knock! Knock!
Who's there?
JESSAMINE.
Jessamine who?
Jessaminute and I'll tell you.

Knock! Knock!
Who's there?
JILL.
Jill who?
Jilly Babies are my favourite thing.

What do you call the boy with the vaulting horse
on his head?
JIM.

There was a young lady called JO
Who wore padding from head down to toe
   She was hit by a truck
   Which was very bad luck —
She's still bouncing as far as we know.

Knock! Knock!
Who's there?
JOANNA.
Joanna who?
Jo an' NATALIE . . .

Knock! Knock!
Who's there?
JOANNE.
Joanne who?
Jo an' JESSICA . . .

Knock! Knock!
Who's there?
JODIE.
Jodie who?
Jo decided to send me, cos she an' Natalie an'
Jessica couldn't get in.

Knock! Knock!
Who's there?
JOE.
Joe who?
Well, I'm not Joe King, that's for sure.

Find the hidden name:
TEACHER: How do you spell 'age'?
BOY: *A.J.*
TEACHER: Oh no! you stupid boy.
          Answer – *JOHN.*

SHE: I like my boyfriends to be frank.
HE: *But my name's JONATHAN!*

There was a young lady called JULIA.
Whose habits were rather peculiar.
    She'd rush down the street,
      On her *hands*, not her feet,
That rather peculiar Julia.

Gigantic Julian: I wouldn't say JULIAN was tall, but the barber has to stand on a ladder to cut his hair!

A teacher was taking her class for a walk in the woods. 'Now, JULIE,' she said, 'what do we call the outside of a tree?'

'I don't know, miss,' said Julie.

'Bark, you silly girl, bark!' said the teacher.

'O.K.' said Julie. 'Woof woof.'

Knock! Knock!
Who's there?
JULIET.
Juliet who?
Juliet my bag of chips.

JUNE: Mum, I don't like this cheese with holes in it.
MUM: *Well, eat the cheese and leave the holes on the side of your plate.*

Knock! Knock!
Who's there?
JUNO.
Juno who?
Course I do!

Knock! Knock!
Who's there?
JUSTIN.
Justin who?
Justin time for tea.

Knock! Knock!
Who's there?
JUSTINE.
Justine who?
Justine old-fashioned girl.

K

Who do get if you cross a motor with a little bird?
KAREN.

What is a monster's favourite English dish?
KATE and SIDNEY pie.

Knock! Knock!
Who's there?
KATHERINE.
Katherine who?
Here we come, Katherine nuts and may.

K is for kind little KATY,
Who weighs near a hundred and eighty.
    She has 10 meals a day
    And her doctors all say
That's the reason that Katy's so weighty.

What girl is lurking inside a 'yak'?
          Answer – *KAY*.

Knock! Knock!
Who's there?
KEITH.
Keith who?
Keith me quick!

TEACHER: KELLY, you copied the answers from FELICITY's paper, didn't you?
KELLY: *How did you know?*
TEACHER: For question 2, her paper says 'I don't know the answer'. Your says 'Neither do I.'

Knock! Knock!
Who's there?
KEN.
Ken who?
Ken't you guess?

Knock! Knock!
Who's there?
KERRY.
Kerry who?
Kerry me inside, I'm half dead out here.

A teacher was talking to a new boy in her class.
    'What's your name?' she asked him.
    He scratched his head and looked puzzled. Then he began to sing. 'Happy birthday to you, happy birthday to you, happy birthday, dear Kevin . . . Please, Miss, it's KEVIN,' he said.

Knock! Knock!
Who's there?
KIRSTY
Kirsty who?
Kirsty when you meet the queen.

L

What is the name of a boy who's confused but 'clean'?

Answer – *LANCE.*

Knock! Knock!
Who's there?
LAURA.
Laura who?
Laura people like the Beatles.

Knock! Knock!
Who's there?
LAUREN.
Lauren who?
Lauren n' Hardy.

MOTHER: LEE, why do you say the teacher's always picking on you?
LEE: *Because whenever there's a row she always says 'Quiet-lee'.*

Knock! Knock!
Who's there?
LEANNE.
Leanne who?
Leanne on me when you are down.

Knock! Knock!
Who's there?
LEONIE.
Leonie who?
Leonie one I think about is you.

'Mum,' said LESLEY, 'Lindsay called me stupid.'
  'LINDSAY,' Mum said, 'tell Lesley you're sorry.'
  Lindsay sighed. 'I'm sorry you're stupid,' she said.

Find the hidden name.
'You won't have time to eat your muesli, lying in bed like that.'
Answer – *LILY*.

Knock! Knock!
Who's there?
LINDA.
Linda who?
Linda hand, I can't get this door open.

Knock! Knock!
Who's there?
LIONEL.
Lionel who?
Lie, an' I'll be furious.

Knock! Knock!
Who's there?
LORRAINE.
Lorraine who?
Lorra rain about today.

What do you call the girl who gets all muddled up when she goes for a 'sail'?
Answer – *LISA*.

Knock! Knock!
Who's there?
LUCINDA.
Lucinda who?
Lucinda chain and let me come in.

'What's your name cowboy?'
'They call me TEX.'
'You must come from Texas.'
'Nope. I come from Louisiana, but I'm darned if they're going to call me LOUISE!'

What do you call the girl with the mower on her head?
LORNA.

What do you call the girl with the unrestrained fishy creature on her head?
LUCILLE.

Knock! Knock!
Who's there?
LUCY.
Lucy who?
Loose elastic lets you down.

Knock! Knock!
Who's there?
LUKE.
Luke who?
Luke outside and see for yourself!

What do you call the girl who wears a pair of lavatory seats as earrings?
LULU.

A skinny young lady called LYNN
Was so unbelievably thin
    That there was no knowing
    Her coming or going,
And she never would tell where she'd bin.

M

Knock! Knock!
Who's there?
MANDY.
Mandy who?
Mandy lifeboats, the ship is sinking.

Who do you get if you put mother in an attic?
MARGARET.

Knock! Knock!
Who's there?
MARIE.
Marie who?
Can't tell you. Ma real name's a secret!

What does a girl do on her wedding day?
MARIGOLD

Knock! Knock!
Who's there?
MARK.
Mark who?
Ma can't cook for toffee.

Knock! Knock!
Who's there?
MARION.
Marion who?
Marion in haste, repent at leisure.

Knock! Knock!
Who's there?
MARIA.
Maria who?
Maria's aching, standing out here in the wind.

What do you call the girl standing with the wedding ring on her head?
MARIANNE.

Knock! Knock!
Who's there?
MARTHA.
Martha who?
Ma thirsts for a cup of tea.

Who do you get if you cross mother with a can of soup?
MARTIN.

What was Santa Claus's wife called?
MARY, of course. Mary Christmas, to you.

What do you call the boy who keeps lying in front of the door?
MAT.

Knock! Knock!
Who's there?
MATTHEW.
Matthew who?
Matthew alwayth thspeak with a listhp?

Knock! Knock!
Who's there?
MAVIS.
Mavis who?
Mavis be the last time I knock on your door!

What do you call the boy who wears two raincoats?
MAX.

Knock! Knock!
Who's there?
MAY.
May who?
May I come in, please?

What do you call the girl who's an absolute 'gem'
but a bit confused?
Answer – *MEG*.

Knock! Knock!
Who's there?
MEGAN.
Megan who?
Megan sure I'm not a burglar?

Who do you get if you cross a fruit with part of your
leg?
MELANIE.

If you should meet MELISSA
You're bound to want to kiss her
And then you'll mope, and miss her,
So . . . don't go near Melissa.

Who do you get if you cross yourself with a mollusc?
MICHELLE.

Knock! Knock!
Who's there?
MIKE and YVETTE.
Mike and Yvette who?
My cat is ill and a vet is coming to see it.

Knock! Knock!
Who's there?
MONICA.
Monica who?
Monica'nt buy me love!

Knock! Knock!
Who's there?
MORAG.
Morag who?
More aggro on the way!

N

Knock! Knock!
Who's there?
NAN.
Nan who?
Nan of my other friends will come out today.

Who do you get if you cross an insect with a narrow street?
NATALIE.

NATHAN is a reggae freak,
He does it all day long.
He concentrates on rhythm
And bangs a bloomin' gong.

There was a young cannibal called NED
Who used to eat onions in bed
    His mother said, 'Sonny,
    It's not very funny,
Why don't you eat people instead?'

What do you call the boy on his knees?
NEIL.

Knock! Knock!
Who's there?
NICK.
Nick who?
'Nickers in a twist.

What do you call the boy who's lost his underpants?
NICHOLAS.

Knock! Knock!
Who's there?
NICOLA.
Nicola who?
Knicker elastic must be strong.

'Who can give me a sentence using the word "fascinate"? asked the teacher. NIGEL's hand shot up. 'Very good,' said the teacher. 'Let us hear it.'

'My coat has 10 buttons,' said Nigel, 'but I can only fascinate.'

O

What do you call the girl with the unpaid bill in her hand?
ODETTE.

Knock! Knock!
Who's there?
OLGA.
Olga who?
Olga home if you don't let me in.

Knock! Knock!
Who's there?
OLIVE.
Olive who?
Olive you too, sweetheart.

Knock! Knock!
Who's there?
OLIVER.
Oliver who?
A liver and bacon sandwich does you good.

Knock! Knock!
Who's there?
OSCAR and GRETA.
Oscar and Greta who?
Oscar foolish question and Greta silly answer.

Knock! Knock!
Who's there?
OWEN.
Owen who?
Owen up, I know you're hiding in there!

P

What do call the boy working in a rice field?
PADDY.

What do you call the tap-dancer who likes dancing backwards?
Answer – *PAT*.

Who do you get if you cross father with a rabbit in a hat?
PATRICK.

Knock! Knock!
Who's there?
PAUL.
Paul who?
Paul the other one, that's got bells on.

Knock! Knock!
Who's there?
PAULA.
Paula who?
Paula pair of wellies on and come out to play.

What do you call the girl with an oyster shell on her head?
PEARL.

What do you call the girl with a washing basket on her head?
PEG.

What do call a lady copper?
PENNY.

Knock! Knock!
Who's there?
PETER.
Peter who?
P to Z is the last bit of the alphabet.

Who do you get if you mix up a puppy, a flower and a note of music?
PETULA.

What do you call the boy with a petrol pump on his head?
PHILIP.

Knock! Knock!
Who's there?
PHILIPPA.
Philippa who?
Philippa bucket of water — your front door's on fire.

Knock! Knock!
Who's there?
POLLY.
Polly who?
POLLY! Put the kettle on.

Knock! Knock!
Who's there?
PRUE.
Prue who?
Proof of the pudding is in the eating.

R

What 7 letters did RACHEL say when she opened the fridge door and saw there was no food inside?
O.I.C.U.R.M.T.

Knock! Knock!
Who's there?
RALPH.
Ralph who?
Ralph! Ralph! I'm a puppy dog.

Knock! Knock!
Who's there?
RAMONA.
Ramona who?
Ramona going to ask you once more. Can I come in?

Knock! Knock!
Who's there?
RAOUL.
Raoul who?
Raoul out the barrel.

What do you call the person with a shaft of sunshine on their head?
RAY.

I sat next to REBECCA at tea,
It was just as I feared it would be,
    Her rumblings abdominal
    Were simply pheomenal
And everyone thought it was me.

Knock! Knock!
Who's there?
REX.
Rex who?
Don't pull all your Rex in one basket.

Knock! Knock!
Who's there?
RHODA.
Rhoda who?
Rhodadendron.

Knock! Knock!
Who's there?
RICHARD.
Richard who?
Richard and you should be able to reach the door
handle.

Knock! Knock!
Who's there?
RINGO.
Ringo who?
Ringo, ringo roses.

What do you call the boy with two oars on his head?
ROBERT.

What do you call the girl who said thank you to the burglar?
ROBERTA.

What do you call the burglar who broke into the pub?
ROBIN.

TEACHER (on telephone): You say ROGER is poorly and can't come to school today? To whom am I speaking?
ROGER (in a grown-up voice): *This is my father speaking.*

Knock! Knock!
Who's there?
ROLAND.
Roland who?
Roland butter for my tea please.

What name did the witch give her cooking pot?
It was called-RON.

What do you call the girl who stood up?
ROSE.

What do you call the girl with the sweet, purple herb on her head?
ROSEMARY.

Knock! Knock!
Who's there?
RUPERT.
Rupert who?
Rupert your left leg out, rupert your left leg in . . .

What do you call the boy who's just slipped head-first into a pile of fallen leaves?
RUSSELL.

There was a young lady called RUTH
Who had a great passion for truth.
    She said she would die
    Before she would lie —
And she died in the prime of her youth.

What do you call the boy who jumbles up his
mother's knitting 'yarn'?

Answer – *RYAN*.

S

Knock! Knock!
Who's there?
SAL.
Sal who?
S'alarming that you don't recognize me.

What did the battery hen farmer call his twins?
SAM 'n' ELLA.

Knock! Knock!
Who's there?
SAMANTHA.
Samantha who?
Sam an' tha rent man. Open up and pay up!

Find the hidden name:
'When you have a picnic on the beach the sand
rather spoils the taste of the sandwiches.'
Answer – *SANDRA*.

What do you call the child with the bucket and
spade on their head?
SANDY.

Knock! Knock!
Who's there?
SARAH.
Sarah who?
Sarah doctor in the house?

Knock! Knock!
Who's there?
SCOTT.
Scott who?
Scott to be *me*, hasn't it?

What do you call the girl who keeps getting mixed
up about 'aliens'?
Answer – *SELINA*.

Knock! Knock!
Who's there?
SETH.
Seth who?
Seth me, that'th who.

TEACHER: SHARON, can you give me a sentence
to explain the meaning of centimetre?
SHARON: *Yes, Miss. My cousin BEVERLEY came
to stay and I was centimetre.*

SHAUN: Who's that at the door?
SHELIA *A man trying to sell a beehive.*
SHAUN: Tell him to beehive himself and buzz off.

Knock! Knock!
Who's there?
SHIRLEY.
Shirley who?
Surely you know!

Knock! Knock!
Who's there?
SID.
Sid who?
Sid down, you're rocking the boat.

Knock! Knock!
Who's there?
SIGRID.
Sigrid who?
Sigrid service – open up!

Knock! Knock!
Who's there?
SIMON.
Simon who?
Simon the mood for love.

What did King Canute say to the waves?
STACEY.

Knock! Knock!
Who's there?
STAN.
Stan who?
Stan' back, I'm knocking the door down.

If STEPHANIE becomes a swot
And does what she is told,
I think she'll find she's missed a lot
When she has grown old.

What do you call a bird walking backwards?
STEPHEN.

Knock! Knock!
Who's there?
STELLA.
Stella who?
Stella you don't open the door to me.

Knock! Knock!
Who's there?
STEWART.
Stewart who?
Stew artichokes to make a tasty supper.

What is SUSAN's favourite pudding?
Su-et

SUZANNE: I wouldn't say SUZANNE is shy, but she goes into the next room to change her mind!

What do you call the girl who always wants to pay in expensive restaurants?
SYBIL.

Knock! Knock!
Who's there?
SOPHIE.
Sophie who?
Sophie-s is where you live.

T

Knock! Knock!
Who's there?
TAMARA.
Tamara who?
Tamara's another day – I'll come back then.

TAMMY: My brother's a maniokleptic
SAMMY: *Don't you mean a kleptomaniac?*
TAMMY: No, he walks backwards into shops and leaves things.

How do you say thanks to the boy with four identical brothers?
TARQUIN.

Knock! Knock!
Who's there?
TERRY.
Terry who?
Terrified out here in the dark!

Knock! Knock!
Who's there?
TERESA.
Teresa who?
Teresa green and sky's blue.

Knock! Knock!
Who's there?
TESSA.
Tessa who?
Tess a coin to decide.

Knock! Knock!
Who's there?
THEO.
Theo who?
The' other day you asked me to call round.

Knock! Knock!
Who's there?
TIM.
Tim who?
T'impossible to tell unless you open the door.

Knock! Knock!
Who's there?
TINA.
Tina who?
Tea 'n' a bun is what I fancy.

Knock! Knock!
Who's there?
TOBY.
Toby who?
To be or not to be: that is the question.

GOTTLE of GEER

Knock! Knock!
Who's there?
TOM.
Tom who?
Tom-a-to soup.

Who do you get if you cross part of your foot with part of your leg?
TONI.

Who do you get if cross an usherette's icecream container with the ocean?
TRACEY.

TREVOR opened the door and saw his teacher standing there.

'Are your parents in?' asked the teacher.

'They was in,' said Trevor, 'but they is out now.'

'They *was* in! They *is* out!' said the teacher. 'Where is your grammar?'

'Oh!' said Trevor. 'She's inside watching the telly!'

Knock! Knock!
Who's there?
TRISTAN.
Tristan who?
Trist and shout!

Knock! Knock!
Who's there?
TROY.
Troy who?
Troy as I might I can't reach the doorbell.

Knock! Knock!
Who's there?
TRUDY.
Trudy who?
Door's locked. I'm coming Trudy window.

What do you call the boy who has his own bicycle business?
TYRONE.

U

Knock! Knock!
Who's there?
UNA.
Una who?
You know who.

Knock! Knock!
Who's there?
UNITY.
Unity who?
Unity sweater for me?

V

What do you call the girl who used to get into a spin and 'rave' about the Beatles?
Answer – *Vera.*

Why did VERONICA put her father in the refrigerator?
Because she wanted ice-cold Pop!

When VICTOR was dining at Crewe
He found a large mouse in his stew.
  Said the waiter, 'Don't shout,
  Or wave it about,
Or the rest will be wanting one too.'

What do you call the girl with the sweet purple plum in her mouth?
VICTORIA.

W

What do you call Cinderella's fairy godmother?
WANDA.

What do you call the boy with the rabbits up his jumper?
WARREN.

Knock! Knock!
Who's there?
WAYNE.
Wayne who?
Wayne-dwops keep falling on my head!

Knock! Knock!
Who's there?
WENDY.
Wendy who?
Wendy red red robin come bob bob bobbin' along.

Knock! Knock!
Who's there?
WERNER.
Werner who?
Werner you going to stop making these terrible jokes?

Who do you get if you cross WILLIAM with a Power Station?
Electricity Bill.

Knock! Knock!
Who's there?
WINNIE.
Winnie who?
Winnie you going to let me in?

Y

Knock! Knock!
Who's there?
YOKO.
Yoko who?
Yoko jump in the lake

Knock! Knock!
Who's there?
YURI.
Yuri who?
Yuri mind me of a broken egg – half cracked.

Z

Knock! Knock!
Who's there?
ZENKA.
Zenka who?
Zenka you for your kind words.

What do you call the girl who got confused because
she 'lazed' in bed all day?
Answer – ZELDA.

Knock! Knock!
Who's there?
ZOE.
Zoe who?
Zo'e upset you? Tell 'im to get lost.